PUBLISHED BY BRENDA COOPER

HALLOWEEN HULLABALOO

ONCE UPON A TIME, A SWEET LITTLE DONKEY
NAMED DIXEY ARRIVED ON A BRAND-NEW FARM
WHERE SHE WAS TO LIVE

ONE SUNNY AUTUMN MORNING, THE ANIMALS
CHATTERED EXCITEDLY ABOUT HALLOWEEN
AS THE LEAVES DANCED IN THE BREEZE.
"HALLOWEEN HULLABALOO!" THEY CRIED,
BUT DIXEY HAD NO IDEA WHAT IT MEANT.

INTRIGUED, SHE DECIDED TO FIND OUT
WHAT IT WAS ALL ABOUT.

DIXEY'S DISCOVERY!

On the new farm, Halloween's in the air.
"Halloween"? Dixey wonders with a curious stare.

Her friends gather 'round; they laugh and say,
"Halloween Hullabaloo's coming our way!"

With pumpkin patches and silly fun to pursue,
Dixey trots off to learn something new.

THE PUMPKIN PATCH ADVENTURE!

To the pumpkin patch, Dixey takes a trot,
With her barnyard friends, it's a delightful plot.

They search for big pumpkins, round and bright,
Carving funny faces making some a fright!

Dixey giggles as she creates her pumpkin's grin,
Halloween's fun; she starts feeling within!

COSTUME CRAZE!

Betty the sheep brings a unicorn horn,
Dixey's dressed up with flowers adorned.

With giggles and laughter, they begin to dress,
Into silly costumes that will undoubtedly impress.

Through the barnyard, they dance, happy and free,
Dixey discovers Halloween is lots of fun, you see.

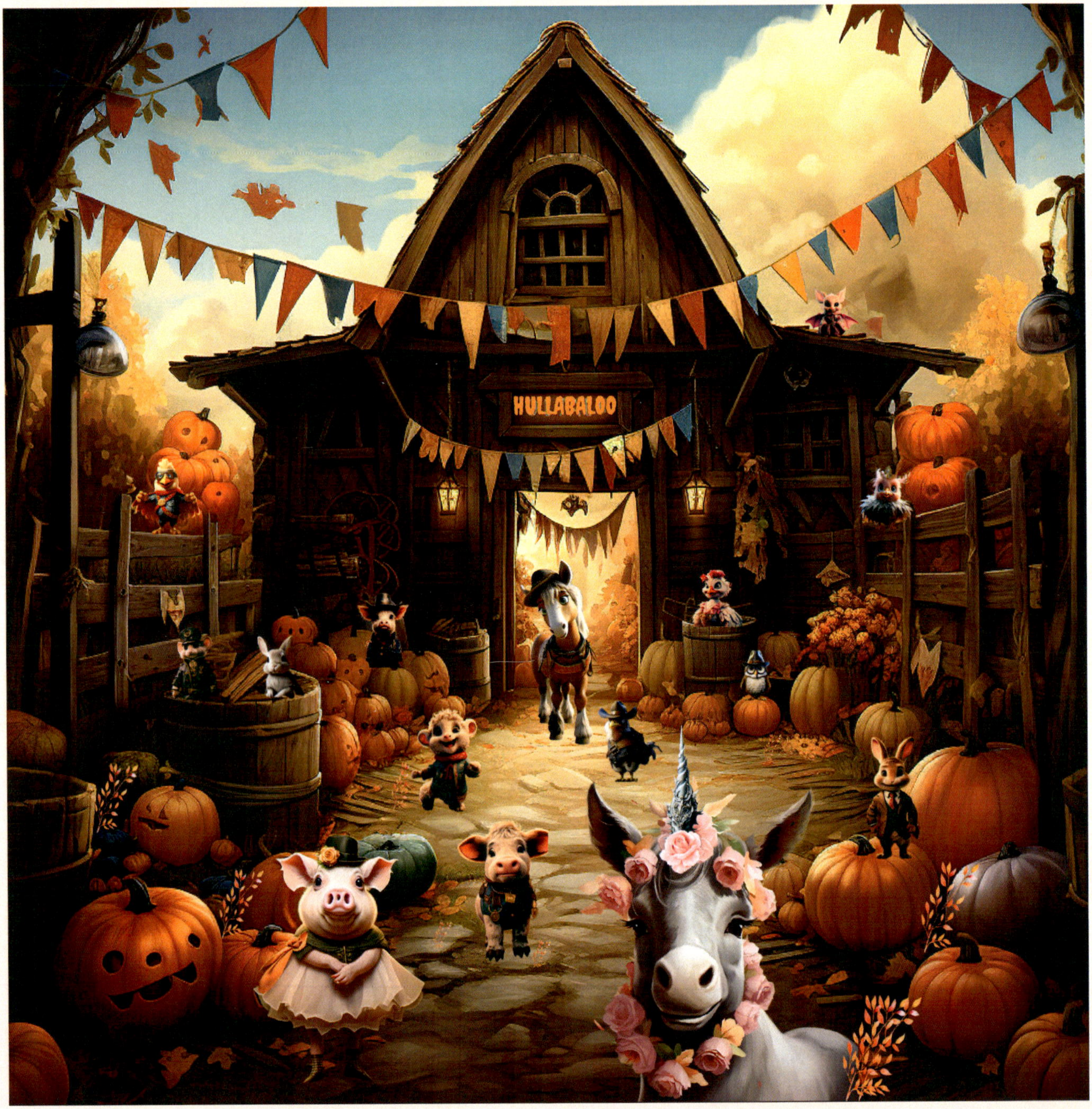
HULLABALOO

SCRITCH, THE GENTLE SCARECROW

In the farmer's field, they find a scarecrow tall,
With a pumpkin head smile, not scary at all.

Scritch welcomes them kindly, with arms open wide,
He laughs and dances with a skip and a stride.

Dixey learns that scarecrows are friendly, not spooky,
Scritch was such a delight—so silly and kooky.

MANDY'S HOMEMADE DELIGHTY

Mandy the Mouse brings treats to share,
Cupcakes with sprinkles—oh, it's so rare!

Dixey bites into a cupcake that is delicious and fine,
With pumpkin frosting, it tastes so divine!

"Thank you, dear Mandy," Dixey said with glee,
Sharing fun times—that's what she can see.

DIXEY'S DISCOVERY!

With Benny the Bunny, they form a big line,
Trick-or-treat, trick-or-treat, they all say in time!

Buckets and baskets, all ready to fill,
Dixey collects candies with a grin and a thrill.

With friends by her side, Dixey feels at ease,
Lots of Hallowen treats with a sugary tease.

LUNA'S SPOOKY TALE

As the sun sets, Luna appears. Oh, so bold,
She tells spooky stories that have never been told.

Of witches and bats and friendly black cats,
Dixey listens closely to Luna the bat.

With Luna's tale done, they look up high,
As the stars twinkle brightly in the darkened sky.

BOBBING FOR APPLES

Rosie the Pig sets up a game to play,
Bobbing for apples with them all on display!

Dixey takes a big bite, a splash, and a crunch,
Halloween is so fun, as she giggles a bunch.

With apples galore, they all have a blast,
Halloween is more fun when worries have passed.

MOONLIT BARNYARD BALL

As the moon rises high, the barnyard comes alive,
They dance and they prance, under the starry sky.

Dixey joins in, feeling giddy and free,
With her barnyard friends, she's as happy as can be.

The night is filled with laughter and cheer,
And now she knows Halloween is not to be feared.

BONFIRE TALES AND TREATS

Around the bonfire, they sit close and near,
Sharing stories and songs with laughter and cheer.

All toasty and warm, they giggle with delight,
Halloween Hullabaloo, it's a fun spooky night!

With hearts so full and smiles so bright,
Dixey's grateful for friends on Halloween night.

A SPECIAL HALLOWEEN

As the morning sun rises, they gather with cheer,
She is grateful for friendships that are so precious and dear.

Dixey's heart is filled with joy and delight,
Halloween on the farm—what a beautiful sight!

With new barnyard friends, she'll never be blue,
For Halloween Hullabaloo, she knows is true.

GRATEFUL HEARTS, FOREVER FRIENDS

And so, Dixey the Donkey's heart was filled with happiness and wonder, knowing that with friends by her side, there was nothing to fear on Halloween anymore. From then on, every year, all her friends on the farm would get together for the most amazing Halloween celebrations, cherishing the friendships they had formed forever.

THE END.

Manufactured by Amazon.ca
Acheson, AB